Heaven AND Earth

by Joan Hutson
Illustrated by Susan Stoehr Morris

CONCORDIA
Publishing House
St. Louis

On earth there are things that make us sad.

In heaven Jesus will wipe away all tears.
There will be no more death or sorrow or pain.
All of that is gone forever.

(Revelation 21:4)

Library of Congress Cataloging in Publication Data
Hutson, Joan
   Heaven and earth.
   (God's little learner series)
   Summary: Contrasts life on earth to that in heaven with Biblical references given for descriptions of heaven.
   1. Heaven—Juvenile literature. 2. Life—Juvenile literature. [1. Heaven. 2. Christian life] I. Title. II. Series.
BT846.2.H87   1985   236'.24   85-7757
ISBN 0-570-08952-2

1 2 3 4 5 6 7 8 9 10   DP   94 93 92 91 90 89 88 87 86 85

On earth we need the sun and the moon for light.

In heaven there is no need for a sun or moon.
The glory of God lights up heaven.

(Revelation 21:23)

On earth we have natural bodies
that can do only natural things.
In heaven we will have spiritual bodies
that will be glorious and powerful.
We will have a body like Jesus' body.

(1 Corinthians 15:43-44, 49)

On earth our minds are sometimes slow
to understand.

In heaven we will understand everything clearly.

(*1 Corinthians 13:12*)

On earth we are sometimes lonely
because we sin and hurt our friends.

In heaven we will never be lonely because
Jesus has forgiven our sins and
has written our names in the Book of Life.

(Ephesians 2:4-6; and Revelation 20:15)

On earth we need night as a time to rest.

In heaven we will need no rest
because we will have perfect, spiritual bodies.

(*1 Corinthians 15:42-43*)

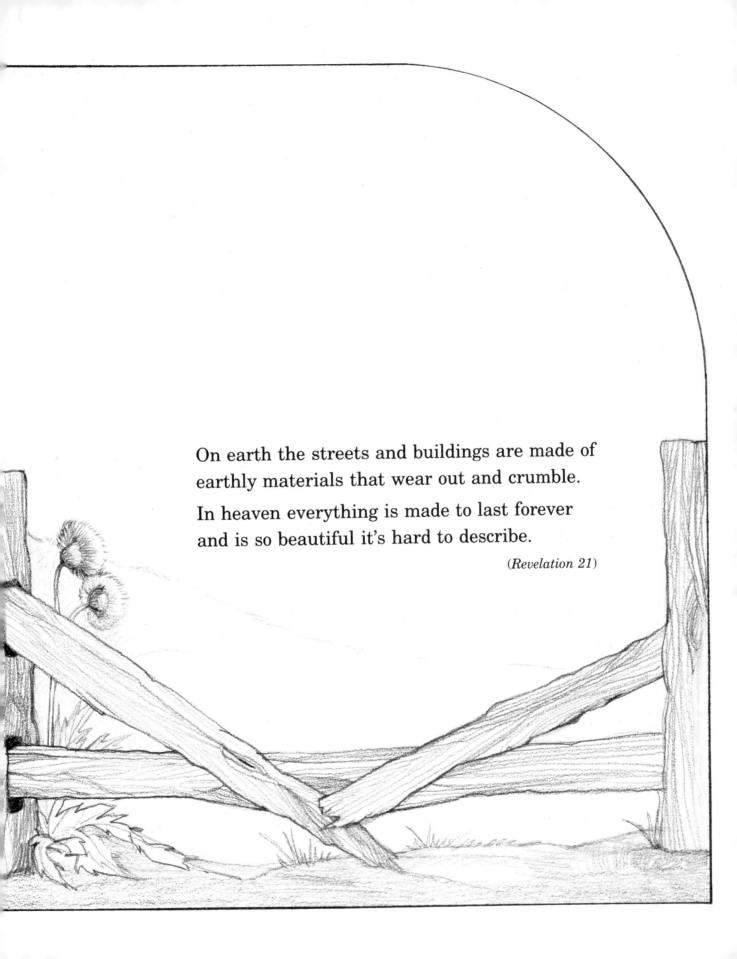

On earth the streets and buildings are made of
earthly materials that wear out and crumble.

In heaven everything is made to last forever
and is so beautiful it's hard to describe.

(Revelation 21)

On earth our rivers are not pure, and
our trees, flowers, and grass wither and die.

In heaven a pure river flows from the throne of God.
There are trees of life that never wither or die.

(Revelation 22:1-2)

On earth some people have poor homes
that are not warm and comfortable.

In heaven Jesus has prepared a place for us
in His Father's many mansions
so that, where Jesus is, we may be also.

(John 14:1-3)

On earth we miss our friends
when we cannot be with them.

In heaven there will be a great reunion of
all the people that ever loved God.

(Hebrews 12:22-24)

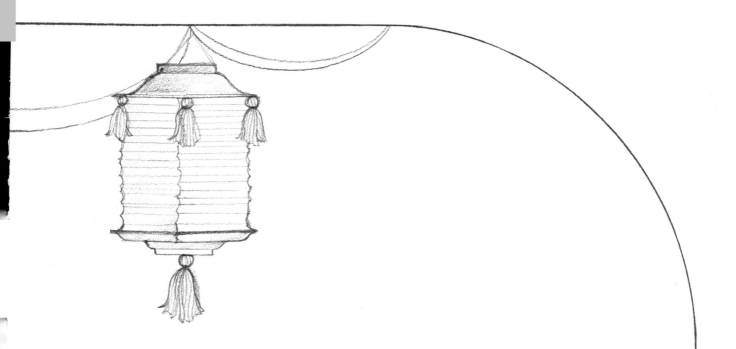

On earth the party and the music ends.

In heaven, our joy and peace and life with God goes on forever and ever.

(Revelation 7:9-17)

THE END